THE REST
YOU KNOW

A MOTHER'S STORY OF SURVIVAL

IRENE W. RUSS

Idea University Press

ISBN 0-9701853-9-1
Library of Congress 2001096966
IUP and Idea University Press are trademarks of GSD&M.
First printing December 2001. Printed in the U.S.A.

THE REST YOU KNOW

FOREWORD

One day about three years ago, I received a package from my mom. I struggled to cut through the FedEx box and bubble pack, and then the extra layer of packaging I've come to expect from my mom. I found a dark, vinyl-covered three-ring notebook.

I opened it up and neatly hand-written on 52 pages of lined high-school notebook paper was my mother's account of the most terrible events of her life: her 14 months as a prisoner in three Nazi concentration camps.

I showed it to several people, including my boss, Roy Spence. He said, "I read your mama's manuscript. I was stunned. I think we're gonna publish it."

Its meticulousness and frankness, its straightforward and vigorous style, is so much more powerful because it doesn't come from a professional writer. It doesn't come from a publicist or a political pundit or even a newspaper reporter. It comes from a four-foot, eight-inch, 77-year-old

Jewish-Hungarian mother, whose story makes her nothing less than a national historic treasure. Moreover, the words are set down just as she put pen to paper.

It was natural that Scott McAfee, my best friend and Mama's favorite, would art direct the book. Thanks to Glenda Goehrs and MaryEllen Rasnick of Idea University Press for helping make this happen. Thanks also to Roy Spence, Judy Trabulsi, Mara Truskoloski, Anne Rix Sifuentez, Diane Patrick, Melissa Padilla, Daniel Rodriguez, Lucy Ray, Kristi Robison and Dorian Girard.

Our whole family would like to offer up Mom's story for posterity and for all the stories that happened there that can never be told.

Daniel Clay Russ
July 2001

My Beloved Children,

For all these years I tried not to think, much less talk bout the past.

But as you were urging me to relate what happened came to realize that I've een very wrong, that you reed to know.

I'm sorry I couldn't articipate in the program f putting my testimony n film. I was asked everal times but each time he nightmares came back.

At least writing it, I could walk away for a while and ome back to it later. Some. imes much later, which is the reason this took me so long.

Once, I heard of a remark
made that what we, from
Hungary suffered doesn't
measure up to the suffering
of those who have been
taken years before.

How do you measure
suffering? By the time spent
in captivity? <u>Not so!</u>

In a blink of an eye,
everything was taken from
us. Family, Friends, Home, our
whole future.

From that moment on,
everything went downhill,
straight into that hell known
as Auschwitz.

That in itself was suffering
enough, to last a lifetime, the
shock of it never leaves you

In the following pages I set down all I could or want to remember.

It is at best a broad outline, it is not possible for me to relate in minute detail the day-to-day occurrences, but all the important things are in there.

Actually I feel better now, I feel as if a lot of my ghosts have been exorcised.

I'll close with my Eternal love to each and every one of you

Mother,

1. THE BEGINNING

I suppose the beginning of the
end for the Jews in Hungary came when
Hungary allied itself with Germany.
I no longer remember the year, but in
the long run it doesn't really matter.

Being young and carefree, I didn't
pay much attention to what was happening outside my little universe until
the restrictions imposed upon the Jews
hit home.

Was it 1942, or even earlier? Some
stores began displaying signs: "Dogs,
Gypsies and Jews not allowed," in that
order.

Then they took the Jewish soldiers out of the regular army units and put them into special work battalions. These then were assigned the hardest, dirtiest tasks.

Some of them were sent to the Russian front, to go ahead of the troops, being used as mine-sweepers. They didn't use mine detectors. They just walked ahead, through the minefields.

Some that survived were captured by the Russians and sent to Siberia. That is what happened to my older brother, Bernard, as we were notified by the Swedish Red Cross. We were still at home at that time. He never came back.

I don't know where my younger brother, David, served, but he came back; he then went to Israel with a transport that left from Italy. The ship he was on was captured by the British, and he spent some time in Cyprus before he was allowed into Israel.

My sister, Jaffa, also came back home, and she left for Israel on another transport that went to Rumania. My brother must have been gone by then, why else would they have gone separately?

I'm just assuming this. They have never explained it to me. My sister still doesn't talk about it.

David died in Israel in 1980. But I'm getting ahead of my story. My father was also called up into

the work camps, but he was released
after a few months, I think because
of his age, but I can't be sure.
While he was away, I had a dream that
it turned out was prophetic.

In the dream I saw two angels,
holding the Safer Torah between them,
surrounded by very bright light, ascend-
ing to the heavens. When my father
came home I told him of my dream. He
just listened and looked very sad.

Then later, just before the German
troops came into Komádi, one night my
father, with the help of some others,
took all the Torah Scrolls and prayer
books out of the Shul and hid them
somewhere.

Before this, there came the restrictions. Being a Jew you could no longer
get a teaching certificate, couldn't
get a license to operate a business of
any sort; however, you could still keep
the ones you already had. At least that
was the case in Komádi; I don't know if
that was the case elsewhere. I have a
feeling some of it depended on the
local "powers that be."

Travel was forbidden. For a while you
could travel with special permission,
but you took the risk of being taken off
the train or bus and summarily deported
to one of the concentration camps. That
happened to one of my friends who was
on her way home from Budapest.

After a time you couldn't travel at all, and after the Germans came we were under a curfew.

On March 19, 1944, Germany occupied Hungary. On March 29 a decree was issued, ordering all Jews to wear the yellow Star of David. Being caught without it was again cause for instant deportation.

The star had to be prominently displayed, at least three inches in diameter of a very bright yellow and had to be sewn onto the garment. To add insult to injury we had to buy our own material and make the stars.

I made dozens of them, for ourselves, as well for others who couldn't. It would have been impossible to put

Main St.
Front Yard
Shul
Flower Garden
Oan House
Wood Shed
Schlacht House
Yard
out house
Yard
shamos
Guest House
Vegetable Garden
Mikvah
Yard
Custodian
Teachers Room
School House
Germans
Play Yard
Back St.

stars on every garment, so we
kept some pieces just to be
worn outside. What others did,
I don't know. There was a large
Jewish population. It could be
that some enterprising people
mass-produced them.

When the Germans came into
Komádi, some of the troops
were quartered in the Shul,
in the schoolhouse, the
teachers' quarters. Of course
school was no longer in
session, the teacher being
away in one of the work camps.
There were Germans in other
buildings as well, as you
can see.

7

In retrospect it is surprising
that they left us pretty much alone.
At times they would just come into the
house, look around and go back out.

Sometimes on Friday evenings some
of them came in to light their ciga-
rettes on the Shabbos candles. One
Saturday morning, an officer came in
while I was still in bed, with the
door closed to my room (we didn't have
so many rooms, but when I was in it,
it was my room). He wanted to know
what was in there. My mother told him
I was asleep and not to disturb me.

He opened the door anyway (who was
to stop him?). I can still see him
standing in the doorway, his thumbs

hooked into his belt, just glaring
at me. He asked what was I doing
still in bed. I said I was trying
to sleep and he would have to leave
and shut the door behind him.

He then said, "How is it, that
you are not afraid of me? When I
speak to my men, their knees are
shaking." I said, "I'm not your
men, my knees are not shaking, now
please leave."

I was so annoyed that it never
occurred to me that he could have
just shot me, but he just turned
and went out.

My poor mother nearly collapsed
from fright.

Once as I passed one of them on the street, he called for me to stop. When I didn't, he shot at me. I felt the bullet go past my ear, but I guess he just wanted to scare me, or maybe he was a lousy shot. When my parents found out about that (from someone else), they hardly ever let me go out again.

Toward the end, some of those living around us would amuse themselves on some mornings just around town, by throwing some kind of exploding pellets at our house. They sounded just like gunfire. That was a pretty harrowing experience.

These are some of the things that stuck in my mind. I am sure there

were other incidents that thankfully
faded from my memory.

Looking back now, I guess they
didn't bother us more than they did
because they knew what fate awaited
us. I don't know what went on with
the other Jews in town, or I just
don't remember anymore — by then we
didn't do much visiting.

We were also pretty much isolated
from the outside world. We no longer
had newspapers delivered to us, which
used to come by mail, as we didn't
have a local paper.

We couldn't own a radio, although
one person had one hidden and listened to it whenever he could and
passed on the news to the rest of us.

So we had some idea of what was happening, but not the magnitude of it.

From what I heard later, mostly there was no warning. The Jews were just taken out of their homes, gathered into ghettoes, and taken to concentration camps.

We in Komádi had some warning, for all the good it did.

Soon after the Germans came to Komádi, the head of the Gendarmes, (the Hungarian Mounted Police we had in Komádi) went to the President of the congregation in the dead of night and told him to prepare us for imminent deportation.

We would be allowed to take one backpack or some such, so after having

made dozens of yellow stars, now I
set to making backpacks for ourselves
as well as for others, because there
were none available in Komádi.

Two days before we were taken,
the Chief of Police, by the same
means, let us know when we would be
taken. He told us to expect it to
happen at night, or very early in the
morning, to take whatever food we
could that wouldn't spoil easily.

This was an extraordinary act of
compassion, considering that had he
been found out, he was assured of
sharing our fate, for anyone trying
to help or comfort, or even to show
pity, was thrown in with the Jews.

I remember my mother making a lot
of shortbread-like cookies. I think
she boiled whatever eggs we could get
and packed bread, potatoes, carrots,
onions. We dug a hole in the storage
room next to the kitchen that had a
brick floor, put our few pieces of
jewelry, photos, etc., in there.

2. TO THE GHETTO

It was end of April or beginning of May, when time ran out for us in Komádi.

They came early one morning. We were herded out of our homes, piled onto (hay?) wagons pulled by oxen. With all the young men away and forced into labor battalions, there were only women, children, older men, the sick — some of whom had to be carried.

We went like the sheep, numbed in shock. How could this be happening? I think that, until then, we didn't really believe that this would actually come to pass. The townspeople must have been ordered to stay indoors. I recall no onlookers.

From the time we got onto the
wagons until I found myself in the
ghetto, I have no conscious memory of
events. My friend, Piri, told me that
we were driven to the edge of town to
a lumberyard (its former Jewish owner
among us), where we spent the night,
waiting for the rest of the Jews from
the surrounding villages.

We were taken to the ghetto in
Nagyvarad. Both my parents had
relatives there whom I had visited
often, but by then they were taken
away. None of them survived. We were
in a stable yard surrounded by a
high wooden fence, the paddocks
filled with Jews, not horses.

People hung sheets between the paddocks
to afford their families some measure of
privacy. I know we slept on the ground,
I don't remember if some straw had been
put down. How and what we ate, water,
sanitation — I can't recall any of it. I
have a vague image of people milling around
what seem to be a few cooking fires.

I buried the memories of those things
for 50 years, and they are now beyond recall, with the exception of the following:

I was with a working party, taken out
of the ghetto to clean houses. I was glad
to be out (under armed guards of course),
even just for a few hours, until I saw
that the houses we were to clean were the
ones the Jews were taken out of. Actually,
we were to sort and clean out their

belongings. Entering the house I was sent
to was like walking into a nightmare.

They must have come for them on a
Friday night, right in the middle of
dinner. There were candlesticks on the
table, plates with half-eaten food on
them, pots on the stove with food still
on them. Even after all these years,
I feel the horror of that experience.

After that day, I always hid when
I saw a working party forming.

The ghetto was situated at a railroad site. I remember seeing the men,
my father among them, periodically
loading boxcars with all kinds of
household goods, which I now know to
have been looted Jewish possessions.

3. TO AUSCHWITZ

On June 26, 1944, we were taken to the rail site and crammed into cattle cars for the trip to Auschwitz. As we were getting on, one of the Germans made me give him my earrings. Little silver bells I had in my ears since I was an infant. I guess I was lucky that he let me take them out myself. All the others had to give up whatever kind of jewelry they still had.

My father and my younger brother Jacob, 13 years old, were pushed into one car. My mother, myself, my sisters (Jaffa 15, Violette 11, Agnes 7 years of age) were together in another car.

I never saw my father or brother
again. Jaffa told me that she saw my
father once through the fence in a pass-
ing work detail. She was on the Auschwitz
side; I was on the Birkenau side.

I don't know how many of us were in
the car. You couldn't sit, couldn't
stretch out or move around. If someone
had to use facilities (buckets in two
corners of the car), people would stand
up to make way, and made a human screen
for privacy. We were on the way for three
days. I don't remember those buckets
being emptied, but I can't be sure.

One man in the car had a couple of
epileptic seizures. It was the first time
I had witnessed one. It was really scary.

My youngest sister ran a fever
throughout that God-forsaken journey.
She was begging my mother to take her
home, give her some chicken soup, so she
could get well. My poor, poor mother.

We may have been given water, I
don't remember. What food we had, we
brought with us from the ghetto.

As time passes, there is not much
conversation. People are more and more
withdrawn. The despair is palpable.

June 29 — The train stopped. The
doors of the car were pulled aside.
We had arrived in Auschwitz, though at
the time I didn't know where we were.
I was just glad that I would be able
to stretch my legs; that gladness
didn't last long. Everyone in our car

arrived alive, which is more than
could be said of some of the other
transports, as I later learned from
some of the others in the camp.

The first glimpse of the outside
showed a bright sunny day, <u>the second,
a line of armed German soldiers facing
the opening doors.</u>

We were quickly bustled out, having to leave our meager belongings
behind. We were to get them later.
Ha! Soon as our feet hit the ground,
the selection began by forming us
into lines as we went.

—<u>Note</u>! Whenever we were lined up,
moved from here to there, it was <u>always</u>
accompanied with yelling, cursing,
shoving, hitting if we didn't move
fast enough. —

Always the guards, armed with
rifles and side arms, the officers
with side arms and swagger sticks,
always the dogs. To this day, just
the sight of a German Shepherd is
enough to throw me into panic.

I don't remember dogs in
Allendorf.

Some of us were directed to the
left, some to the right. My sister,
Jaffa, went with me one way (I don't
remember left or right). My mother
with my two little sisters the other
way. By the time I realized they were
not with us and looked around for
them, I couldn't see them anymore.
I didn't know it then that they were
gone forever.

The group my sister and I were
with was herded into a wire fenced
area. We were facing a building with
a shed-like front. To our right,
beyond the fence, was another fenced
enclosure with mountains of clothing,
luggage, etc. I know now that they
were the last of the belongings of
the Jews, taken off the trains.

In the enclosure with us were
lots of soldiers. Also male prisoners
in black-and-white striped clothing.
These prisoners were part of the
"Sonder Kommando," the special
squads, who did all the dirty work.
They had to extract the gold-capped
teeth of those gassed, put the bodies
into the ovens, etc., etc.

Then an officer stepped forward,
directing those under 16 years of age
to form a separate line. They were to
be given lighter work. Jaffa didn't
want to go, but I talked her into
joining the line. I wanted her to have
it as easy as possible. I didn't realize that she would be taken elsewhere.

We were then ordered to take off
all our clothes!

At first, we were very reluctant
to do that with all the men there, but
with some loud and forceful urging we
did it. They were used to it; we were
not looked upon as human beings. We
were then taken and our hair, head and
body, shorn by said male prisoners.

After that, we were to shower (no
towels), be dusted with disinfectant
and given a garment to put on, which had
to come from the piles of confiscated
clothing. Some of us got a dress, some
a nightgown, some a bathrobe, whatever.
They must have had some fun doing
this. No underwear. I don't remember
if I got some kind of shoes that time.

We were then taken into the camp
itself. Over the entrance was a huge
arch (not McDonald's), with the leg-
end, "Arbeit Macht Frei," meaning,
"Work Brings Freedom." What a joke.
I wonder if even the Germans believed
that. Once inside, we encountered some
Germans sitting at a long table, where
we were registered.

Then each of us was given a post-
card, told to write to anybody back
home saying: arrived safely, I am
well. The postmark said "Waldsee," a
fictitious place.

I don't remember if first we
stood for "Zähl Appell" (standing in
lines to be counted), or were just
told which one of the barracks we
were to sleep in, and turned loose
within the confines of electrified
fences and guard towers.

The wooden barracks had windows on
the sides, one door, wood floor, no
bunk beds as in some other camp areas
(where my sister was, the barracks
had three-tier bunks), no lights. As
I passed one of the windows, I saw my

reflection and turned around, thinking there was someone behind me. I didn't recognize myself. We slept on the bare floors, packed like sardines. If someone wanted to turn over, the whole row had to turn. We were locked in at night, so they put a bucket in to use if needed.

There was a clinic in the compound, but to go there with any complaint meant an almost sure ticket to the gas chambers.

For facilities, we had an open ditch with a plank over it. There we had to squat in plain sight. (We didn't even have a Sears Catalog.)

The book about Auschwitz mentions
covered latrines and wash houses. Not
where I was. The only time we had a
chance to wash was when periodically
we were taken to the showers. Other
times I would save a few drops of my
drinking water to wash my face.

Having been processed and turned
loose, I set about looking for my
mother and sisters (not my father and
brother, this being a woman's camp)
and not finding them.

Some of the inmates already there
said that I might as well forget
about them, that if they were not
already dead, they would soon be, and
that we also were either to be worked
to death or killed outright.

Thinking back on that first day, I see only the desolation of my mind and spirit. Just as if a switch had been pulled, my thoughts and feelings shut down. From that time until I was liberated, all conscious emotions left me. I lost all hope and with it all fear. Nothing could touch me anymore.

In addition to the passage of years, my lack of memory of some happenings is partially due to the above described condition, which in turn may have helped preserve some of my sanity.

A typical day in the camp started by being rousted out of the barracks way before daylight. We lined up to be counted in three rows, each block

(barracks) separately. There were a
number of guards and "Aufseherin"
(woman overseers) counting us. Some
from front to back, others from back
to front. This went on for hours at a
time. When they finally reconciled
their numbers, we were given what
passed for coffee.

This process was repeated again
in the evening, after which we were
fed. We were each given a small pot
or bowl to receive our food in. No
eating utensils of any sort. You kept
this dish with you all the time; if
you lost it you were out of luck.

Our meal was some watery slop,
into which they put something which
stopped our periods. That in itself

was a blessing under the circumstances.
Also a piece of bread and sometimes a
piece of salami of horse meat. For two
days I ate nothing but the bread and
coffee, because it wasn't kosher. After
that I didn't care.

Occasionally they put a bucket of
water into the barracks. There was never
enough of it. I remember trying to catch
some rainwater one day in my little pot.

We didn't work. We spent the day
between morning and evening "Appell"
just milling around, or sitting trying
to keep away from the guards. Just
marking time.

When we were packed in for the
night, the "Aufseherin," the woman

overseer, came in, picking her way
between us with her dog — whip always
ready — for a last check of the day
before locking us in for the night.
There were woman supervisors in each
of the barracks, who were responsible
for peace and order among the inmates.
These women were prisoners, even
meaner than the Germans if that is
possible; but it is almost under-
standable, since their lives were on
the line.

And so it went day after day,
with the exception of the few times
we were taken to the showers, which
as you can imagine, we were badly in
need of. Each time we were dusted
again and given another rag to wear.

Each day, some of the women took huge pots (of soup?) over to the Auschwitz side. One of them ran into Jaffa, and one time she let me take her place to give me a chance to see my sister for a few minutes. I saved my little piece of bread from the night before, so I could give her something. She looked so pitiful that, had I had any feeling left in me, I surely would have gone mad.

It was 25 years before I saw her again. We could do this substitution, because we all looked the same to the Germans. All that mattered was that the numbers (we were always counted) were the same going out and coming back in.

Toward the middle of August (at the time I didn't know the date), we were again taken to the showers, after which we were paraded <u>naked</u> past a long table where German officers were seated. Flanking them were the armed guards with the dogs. — Much later I heard that one of them was Mengele. I really didn't think that any of us knew at the time who or what he was. —

I'm now sure that the afore-mentioned trips to the showers were not due to the Germans' concern for hygiene. Instead they preceded further selections. Just as it happened when I was picked for Allendorf. The day before, another transport was sent

off, including most of the women from
Komádi. I so wanted to go with them,
but how fortunate I was not to have
been included. Those poor souls were
put on road work and all but a few
died. One of them got back to Komádi;
but I heard that she became mentally
unbalanced.

The selection of 1,000 women
completed, we were each given a thin
short-sleeved gray dress, our prisoner
number on the sleeve. My number was
25956. I was given some kind of shoes,
no sox. Some of the others had wooden
shoes. I still don't remember underwear.
Having been so royally outfitted, we
were separated from the other inmates.

The railroad went right through,
or was next to, Birkenau. We spent
part, or all of the night, in a field
next to the railroad. I remember eating cabbage stubs under the cover of
darkness. Were we really in a cleared
cabbage patch? Or was the cabbage
given to us? Or was I so hungry that
I dreamed the whole thing?

4. TO ALLENDORF

As for getting on the train —
again cattle cars, complete with
buckets — I have no memory. Nor do I
remember how long we were under way.
I'm sure it took several days.
Allendorf, looking at the maps, seems
to be quite a distance from
Auschwitz. Were we fed, given water?
Probably so, as we were being taken
to work, though I didn't know that at
the time. The only clear memory I
have of that whole trip is the train
stopping in Weimar.

When the doors were pushed aside,
across some tracks in front of the
depot, were people apparently waiting
for a train. We were gazing in amaze-
ment at the women wearing hats,
gloves, hose, and were nudging each
other — Did you see the hat, gloves,
etc.? — as if we just had come out of
the jungle. What they did to us in
such a short time. It is the only time
I remember the doors to be opened on
the cattle cars: when the train
stopped at a station, probably only to
let us empty the slop buckets into the
station's facility, for which task I
was volunteered.

Engraved in my mind's eye is a
picture of this: I'm barefoot, carrying

the two buckets, being escorted by a
German guard armed with a rifle and
side arm. As if I were going anywhere!
Why is this picture still so vivid?
Was it more degrading with the civilians looking on than other — worse —
indignities that were visited upon
us, that were witnessed only by other
inmates and our captors? Who knows?

Now, we are in Allendorf. Here,
the barracks had rooms. I don't know
how many. The room I was in had six
sets of double bunk beds, a straw
mattress on each and one blanket.
Seems like there was a table. (Were
there chairs?) There was a wood-
burning stove, but we never had anything to burn in it.

One time, when one of the women was sick with chills and fever and it was bitter cold in the room, some of us decided to steal some wood out of a woodshed, where broken bunks and such were kept. This was in the winter, of course. I don't know how we hoped to light a fire — we had no matches. Maybe we thought we could get some from somebody in the kitchen. As it happened, we didn't have to worry about it, because we got caught, and for several nights we had to stand guard at the woodshed — two hours on, two hours off.

Finally, I guess, the Aufseher got tired of getting out every two hours to tell us to change the guard, because we had no way to tell the time. After a few nights he let us off. Everything considered, that was a pretty mild punishment. But wasn't it enough punishment, just to be there? The usual punishment for breaking the rules was to have your hair cut off again and be locked in a cell, and/or having to stand at Appell for however long it pleased them.

We were given one hot meal a day of potato soup, sometimes with carrots. It was hot, and sometimes, it seems to me, there were flecks of meat in it, but don't make book on that. We had this meal in the mess

hall, sitting on benches at tables.
Those of us working in the factories
were given one glass of milk a day, to
counteract the poison we were working
with and breathing in every day. The
rest of our rations consisted of a
piece of very coarse dry bread, one-
third of an eight-inch by four-inch
loaf, approximately, also a piece of
salami, about two inches, of horse
meat, and a pat of margarine. This may
have been given to us each day, I
don't remember. This was apportioned
to us by one of the women picked from
our midst, who was also responsible
for everything that happened in our
barrack.

There was a clinic, I don't know
how it was appointed. I never had to
visit it. A shed with running water
(cold), where you could wash and wash
your dress. We were given a hot shower.
I don't recall if it was weekly or
bi-weekly. Two people shared a coarse,
loosely woven towel, approximately
thirty-six inches by eighteen inches.
Each of us was very careful to use
only half of it.

We were given small bars of very
coarse soap, grey in color, which we
were never told after liberation were
made of Jewish fat, though now it was
said. There is not enough documentation
to prove it. I had two partially used
bars and two unused bars that were

given to your Father in Stettin by
a German ex-soldier, who told him he
worked where the soaps were made.
I kept them, not knowing what to do
with them, until one day in 1970
I gave them to Rabbi Feldman, who
buried them in Greenwood Cemetery at
the foot of the Holocaust Memorial.
As I was getting ready to attend the
burial, I had a vision of rows upon
rows of the dead. I could not go to
the burial, and wasn't able to visit
the grave until May 1996.

That year, Lola Larvsyk, Helen
Gerson's sister, had the Henrshech
(sic) (an organization of the
Holocaust survivors) put up a plaque

for my lost family on the roll of the
Memorial. Because of that, I had to
go to the cemetery to the Memorial
Service on Yom Hashoah, The Day of
Remembrance, to see the Plaque and
visit the little grave.

- - - - - - - - - - - - - -

    The factory was about seven
kilometers (?) from the camp. The way
to it was through woods. I guess the
factory was hidden by them. The air
had an all-pervasive bitter almond
smell to it; you could almost taste
it. It turned leaves on the trees
yellow. We had a little grey head
scarf. It also turned yellow. Some
were sickened by it. I was one of the

lucky ones to escape its effect.
Incredibly, there was only one death,
as I recently learned, due to TNT poi-
soning. I think we worked 12-hour
shifts. It was dark, going to work and
coming back. We walked at a fast pace,
always urged on by the guards yelling
and cursing, mostly by the women guards.

The first place I was assigned to
was a very large room, which had two
huge vats in it. The room was self-
contained — the only way in or out was
by the freight elevator. There were
four of us working in there, two to
each vat. An elderly Wermach was our
supervisor. He treated us kindly;
sometimes he even shared his lunch
with us.

Our job was to pour four sacks of
two (?) kinds of powdery material
into the vats. Those sacks were very
heavy. It took two of us to lift
them. These were replenished several
times during our shift. Fortunately
they came up on the elevator. It was
enough just to drag them to vats.

Our supervisor watched us closely
filling the vats, to be sure we used
the proper proportions, and cautioned
us not to ever mix them up. I now
wonder if there were more than two
kinds of stuff that he was so concerned about accuracy? When the stuff
we poured in got mixed, there was a
signal and the old man opened a tap

above the vats and let some greenish-
yellow liquid pour into the vats.
This deadly mixture went to fill the
bombs, shells, etc., below. When the
vats emptied, the whole process was
repeated. After a time, when he was
satisfied that we knew how to do the
pouring, he removed himself to a
cubicle in the far corner of the room
near a window, and came out only to
release the liquid. I now think he
just wanted to be away, to keep from
breathing in the fumes. There had to
be some nasty stuff floating around
in the air, because in all the time I
worked there, we never had any of the
SS coming to check on us, as they did
in other areas.

Anyway, his leaving us unsupervised
gave us a chance to try a little sabotage.
Every so often we would do a musical
sacks number, thoroughly mixing up the
sacks, hoping to produce a few duds.

Next I was sent to drill holes in the
filled bombs/shells (?). I don't really
know what they were. It seems they were
about 30 inches long, about 10 inches in
diameter. I never paid attention to the
size of them, nor the weight, which I
hear was around 100 pounds. It's hard
even to estimate after all this time and
some of the numbers I hear from others
(prisoners).

We had to lift them onto the drill by
hand, on a conveyor belt, which took them

to a German, who measured the depth of
the hole drilled. I suppose that is
where the detonator was installed.
Each drill was numbered and each bomb
had to be marked, to show which drill
it came from. The drill I worked with
was operated with a lever, something
like the slot machines used to have.
Most of the others were controlled by
a wheel. Once, my machine developed a
problem, and they called in a mechanic.
He was a Czech prisoner of war, and
while he was working on the machine,
he showed me how to control the lever
where it wouldn't drill to the correct
depth, and even to put it out of
commission altogether.

So then I did some sabotage on
the drill, as often as I dared, until
one day, this SS officer stopped by
my work stand and demanded to know
why my drill produced so many useless
bombs. I told him he needed to get me
a new drill, if he expected me to do
better. It's a wonder that he didn't
just shoot me right there.

From there, I was sent to steam-
clean buckets full of nuts (as in
nuts and bolts) of some caked-on
substance with a leaky hose. The nuts
were taken off the duds.

Next stop; I'm climbing up in a
giant flue scraping the inside of it
— yellow, bitter-tasting dust flying

as I scrape. Now, I see myself up on
a catwalk working on what probably
were rockets or torpedoes. What was
I doing with them? The factory I was
working in was built to fill these
things and also the bombs, etc., so I
was probably working on filling them.
There was another factory nearby,
where I think they were manufactured.
I have no idea how long I have worked
at any one place.

When the weather turned cold, we
were given a coat. I'm sure they were
part of the plunder, because no two
were alike. The one I got was a nice
tailored Herringbone, with a welt down
the back. A welt is a wide double

seam that is open on the bottom. One
evening on the way back to camp, all
of a sudden I felt like something was
crawling up and down my back. Once
back in the barracks, I laid the coat
on my bed and out comes "UGH" a mouse.
I don't have to tell you that I couldn't
put that coat on again. I traded with
another girl, who was glad to get it.
Hers wasn't nearly as good.

There were some talented people in
the camp, of them a concert violinist,
one an opera singer. The good memory
I have of that time is when they
gathered us in the mess hall to hear a
concert by these two. This was a one-
time occasion. They must have had to

entertain the Germans all along,
otherwise where would the violin have
come from?

Also, there is a sculpture at the
Documentation Center in Stadtallendorf,
by one of the former inmates.

All of a sudden, work stopped at
the factory. This was in early March.
By then, the Kommandant had left the
camp. He was an SS officer. Later
there were rumors that he committed
suicide, leaving his second-in-command
with orders to evacuate the camp.

We were supposed to start marching
to one of the exterminating camps.
This I found out later. Instead, he
found us all kinds of busy work

around the camp, even taking groups
of us into the forest, where we would
pick up fallen limbs, sticks, and
move them from here to there, rake
leaves, etc.

Toward the end of March, when the
American Forces were approximately
only 30 kilometers away, he had to
move us out.

5. THE ROAD TO FREEDOM

Early one morning we left the
camp on foot. We marched all day.
That night we were put up in some
barns. We had only a piece of bread
that we brought with us from the
camp. When we woke up in the morning,
we found ourselves alone, not a guard
in sight. I don't remember seeing any
of the civilians either. We spent the
day in the barn, afraid to move
around. When darkness came, we broke
into small groups and started out. My
group had about two dozen women.

We met some civilians on the road
who told us we should turn around,

because we were headed straight for
the American lines, which was exactly
what we were hoping to do. The road
ran along some heavily wooded hills
and we thought it prudent to get up
there, off the road. Looking down, we
saw German soldiers on foot, retreat-
ing. What a beautiful sight that was.
We walked along for awhile. When we
got tired, we stopped and slept in
the woods.

Next morning we walked out of the
woods and found ourselves in an open
field. We kept parallel to the road;
there was no traffic or people on the
road. About mid-afternoon we saw the
outskirts of a village across the

road. A little further on we saw the
shell of a solitary building in the
middle of the field. It had no roof,
just holes where a door and windows
would have been. As we were very
tired, we decided to take shelter
there. This was late in the afternoon
and we were weak from hunger. I don't
know when we ate last. A couple of the
women decided to go into the village
to see if they could get us some food
and water. We were in luck — they
came back with bread and cheese, and
I guess some water, too.

We spent a very restless night.
We heard planes and explosions. The
railroads were bombed nearby. Finally

things got quiet and we fell asleep.

When morning came, we woke up to loud

clanking noises coming from the road.

Very cautiously we looked out and were

greeted by the most beautiful sight

this side of heaven: those beautiful

tanks with the white star coming down

the road. Some troops walking alongside

them. I wish that I had the ability to

describe my feelings when I saw them.

That first sight of our liberators

is a picture that stays with me always.

Some of the women started running

toward them, the rest of us following

more slowly. When they saw us, the

column halted and some soldiers came

to meet us. They must have met up with

some of the other groups before they came upon us, because they knew who we were. The officer in charge, I'm sure with an escort, went onto Leimsfeld, the village where we were liberated, and brought the Burgermeister (Mayor) with him.

They took us into the village and put us in some dormitories, then food was brought to us by the townspeople. We also received some field rations from the Americans. Some of the troops stayed until they were sure we will be well looked after. So we came under the sheltering arms of the American Occupation Forces.

After a short time, we were placed into private homes, I'm sure by order of the Military Government. Piri, my friend from Komádi, myself and another woman were given two rooms in the home of an old couple, the man having been an old schoolteacher, who was not allowed to teach under the Nazi regime. They treated us very well, even fed us from the very first. We were taken care of by the Military Government, the Red Cross and the UNRRA (United Nations Refugee Relief Agency). They gave us clothes, shoes, etc., money — I don't remember how much. They took care of our medical and dental needs.

We also received ration cards,
because so many things, meat, clothing,
etc., were rationed. The three of us
gave our food ration cards to the
family where we lived, since we took
our meals with them. There being one
kitchen, it made things much simpler.
Besides we didn't have to bother
cooking for ourselves. In addition,
we received care packages every month
either from the UNRRA, or the Red
Cross, I don't remember which.

This continued until circumstances
changed for individual DPs either by
immigrating, returning to their homeland,
or by marriage to someone who wasn't a
Displaced Person. Everybody was at

loose ends; we were just hanging
around, trying to get back into a
semblance of a normal life. We spent
a lot of time going to different
towns when we heard of survivors, to
see if we could find family or
friends. I speak in plural, because
we seldom went anywhere alone.

As you know, I found no one.

Sometime during the year (1945),
the Americans provided transport for
those of us who wished to go back to
Hungary. Piri, my friend, was among
those who decided to go back, so I
packed my meager belongings and went
with them to the train station.
However, when it was time to get on

the train, I changed my mind, thinking: what was there to go back to? I
had no desire to live in Hungary
after they sold us out to the
Germans. To my knowledge I no longer
had anyone there, plus the Russians
occupied the country. I certainly had
no wish to live under Russian rule.

After Piri left I was the only
one living in Leimsfeld. It was the
first time I was left all alone. I
was lonely and felt lost, because
after we were liberated, for a while
I couldn't make myself leave my room,
so Piri took care of things for me.
Even after it got to where I could
function, she kept on helping me, and

we went everywhere, did everything together. So, I went to Ziegenhain just a few miles away (that is where I got married), and got a room there. There were still a lot of us from Allendorf, and others from different camps.

Now, I had to start thinking about where I was going to settle down, for surely I wasn't going to stay in Germany. I applied to immigrate to Israel (then Palestine) because I had an uncle there or the U.S.A., whichever came through first. I never heard from either.

Later I heard that my brother, David, and my sister, Jaffa, were in Komádi. There was a program to send

children to the U.S., not having to
wait for the Quota, and it was
arranged that my sister be included,
if I could get her to come back to
Germany. Just then, a friend from
Komádi came to see me, and he agreed
to go and bring her out of Hungary.
However, by the time he got there
both my sister and brother left
Komádi for Israel (Palestine).

While in Hungary Piri got married
(none of her family survived), so in
the spring of 1946 she and her husband
came back to Germany so they would
have a chance to immigrate somewhere.
I was very glad that they were back.
Again, they took me under their wings

and in effect became my family.
Around that time Zoli and Erma also
came out of Hungary. They settled in
a DP camp near Munich. I went to see
them there. After a while they came
to live in Ziegenhain.

In June, one of the girls got
married. I didn't know her too
well, but everybody was going to the
wedding, so, for the lack of something better to do, I went along.
At the wedding I met your Father.
He knew the Bridegroom, a young
Hungarian DP who worked at the air
base. Once introduced, he (your
Father) didn't leave my side, and at
Piri's urging I agreed to see him

again. Then he began to spend all his free time with me. We were always well chaperoned. Even though we thought that the sun rose and set on the Americans, still and all, he was a soldier and a stranger.

I was staying with Piri and Bela (her husband), and it seemed like he was courting all of us. He would bring foodstuff and other things that weren't available at the German Markets. He was helpful in other ways, too. One of our friends was confined to bed in the Military Hospital near Ziegenhain, due to tuberculosis she contracted in camp. He would often take us out to see her.

I don't remember if he worked at the
motor pool or just knew everybody, but
he could always get a Jeep. (We even
had the use of the Military Governor's
Mercedes on the day of our wedding.)

Anyway, this girl had been waiting
for over a year to be sent to a
Sanitarium in Switzerland. She was
released to Horonerty and Margarenten
(as in Matzo, etc.) I don't remember
which one. As the agencies that were
supposed to work on her case were
dragging their feet, your Father got
in touch with her relatives and was
instrumental in helping them get the
girl to the Sanitarium. They were very
grateful. They wrote your Father a
beautiful letter, offering him any

help should he need it. Before Pesach,
in '47, they wrote that a package with
Passover products was on the way to us,
but it never arrived.

He helped others, too, whenever
he could. We all thought he was the
kindest, most caring person. Once he
expressed a wish to see the factory
where we worked, so Piri, Bela and I
went with him to Allendorf trying to
find the factory. We started out at
the campsite and followed the road we
thought led to the factory, but we
couldn't find it, even though there
were no turn-offs on the road.

The checkpoint, where we were
clocked in and out of the factory, was
gone, and we had no other point of

reference. As I said before, the road
went through the woods. We were always
led, it seems like always in darkness.
I don't wonder we couldn't find it.
We were debating if we should stay in
the town of Allendorf to ask if someone
could help us find the factory, but
decided against it. We didn't think anybody would own up to knowing anything
about the factory because at that time
everybody professed ignorance of the
horrors that were visited upon our
millions. As far as I was concerned, it
was just as well that we didn't find the
factory. I had no great desire to see
it again. I was just happy to have that
chapter in my life closed. However, for

years I was plagued by nightmares,
but at least I could wake out of them.

As we were seeing each other all
the time, we began thinking of the
possibility of marriage. I couldn't,
in all honesty, say that I was madly
in love, but he (your Father) seemed
so good and kind, and I liked him well
enough to accept his proposal of
marriage. He then put in a request for
permission to marry. After I was
investigated and interviewed, permission
was granted. We were married in October
1946: first on October 7 at the regis-
trar's office in Fritzlar, in order to
have quarters assigned in time for the
religious ceremony on October 20.

We were given a house in Ziegenhain, where we lived until an apartment became available on the military compound in Fritzlar.

One funny note: After the ceremony, we had some soup and challah, then we left the wedding party to visit our friend at the hospital as she couldn't attend. By the time we rejoined our guests, there was no food left. When we got home that evening we were both starved. The only things edible in the house were some sardines, onions and crackers. So that's what we had for a wedding feast.

We left Germany from Bremenhaven late December '47, on the troopship

E.B. Alexander. After three-and-a-half
years, I was very happy to shake the
dust of Germany off my feet. Those of
us with children under two years of
age (Harvey was just under 6 months
old), were given cabins on the top
decks. I shared a cabin with another
woman and her child. We had a private
bathroom with a shower. Do you know
that it's very hard to generate soap-
suds in sea water? There was a public
bath with fresh water somewhere on
deck, but I preferred to use the one
we had, even though I had to work a
little harder at it. Your Father, along
with the other married and single men,
was quartered somewhere else.

We arrived at Fort Hamilton (NJ?) January 2, 1948. Somehow, I formed a mental image of seeing flowers everywhere upon my arrival. However, we arrived just after 25 inches of snow fell in the area. All I saw was snow.

After debarkation we were taken to a huge waiting room. We were waiting there to be taken to some sort of lodging, where we would stay until we were processed and your Father got his new orders. All of a sudden there were Aunt Madelyn and Uncle Harry (may they rest in peace). They insisted that we stay with them. Your father accepted the invitation and cleared it with the powers that be.

Big mistake!!! I'm not going to go into
details, but that was a miserable 10
days until your Father finally got his
orders and we could leave NY for
Atlanta.

Your Father had 30 days furlough.
After 30 days in Atlanta, he had to
respond back. He was going to be
stationed at McDill Field, Florida,
near Tampa. He got us an apartment in
Clearwater, where Jeff and Mae Elliot,
who were his longtime friends, lived.
Jeff was the Chief of Police there.
Stephan was born in Clearwater. However,
when I moved down there, your Father
was sent to Augusta, Georgia, to a
military Hospital to have his knee

operated on, that he injured earlier.
Upon his recovery he was discharged
and joined me in Clearwater. We lived
there for about a year.

We came back to Atlanta in the
middle of 1949 and he enrolled at
Georgia Tech. I've been here ever
since, with the exception of the time
I worked in Albany.

The rest you know.

Irene's family, clockwise from left:
Irene, Benzion, Jacob, (Mother) Ethel, Jaffa and
David; only photo of Irene's father, Rabbi Herma▮
Wieder; Jaffa and Kalman Rosenblatt; Jacob Wi▮

Marvin E. Russ

Clockwise from left: Irene, 1945;
Staff Sergeant Marvin Russ, U.S. Army Air Corps;
David Wieder in Israel, 1947;
Marvin and Irene on a date, 1946

Clockwise from left: Rotund Marvin as Santa at U.S. Army barracks in Germany; Irene during performance in acting troupe; wedding day, October 20, 1946

ockwise from left:
arvin and Harvey, 1947;
arvey, Estelle and
ephan, 1956; Barry,
ne and Daniel, 1996;
ne and Estelle, 1956;
ephan, 1951.

side cover front row:
ephan, Harvey; Back
w: Irene, Barry, Estelle,
niel, Marvin, 1958.

AFTERWORD

Irene Wieder Russ was born in Felsozsoltsa, Hungary, in 1924. She lives in DeKalb County, Georgia. Marvin Russ, Irene's husband, died in 1975 from complications resulting from a surgical procedure.

Harvey Russ and Ann, his wife, live in Canton, Georgia. Harvey is a freelance IT manager. Stephan Russ, a noted chef, currently lives in Germany. He has three children. Estelle Erlanger has lived in Jerusalem for 30 years and is married to Rabbi Meyer Erlanger. She has 11 children and four grand-children. Barry Russ and his wife, Jeanne, live in Mableton, Georgia. Barry is an accomplished fashion jewelry designer. Daniel Russ lives with his wife, Caroline, in Austin, Texas. Daniel is a copywriter.